CHAP...

1
THE TRAVEL BASICS
~ page 2

2
GUATEMALA
~ page 5

3
BELIZE
~ page 9

4
EL SALVADOR
~ page 13

5
HONDURAS
~ page 17

6
NICARAGUA
~ page 21

COSTA RICA
~ page 25

8
PANAMA
~ page 29

9
HOSTEL HACKS
~ page 33

10
EXPLORING ADVICE
~ page 35

11
GENERAL TIPS & TRICKS
~ page 37

12
STEPHEN'S SPANISH BASICS
~ page 41

EACH COUNTRY CHAPTER WILL FEATURE AN OVERVIEW OF THINGS TO DO, ACCOMPANIED BY
QUICK FACTS AND MY PERSONAL PICTURES TAKEN WHEN EXPLORING THE COUNTRY

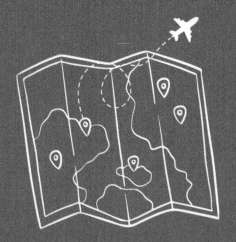

CHAPTER ONE

TRAVEL
BASICS

"The Know How Before the Go How"

I've compiled a quick list of essentials for you to bring. When possible I'll give you my personal tips to get the most out of these necessities!

Passport and Visa: Make sure your passport is valid for at least six months beyond your planned return date. Research visa requirements for each country you intend to visit and obtain them in advance. For readers from Western Countries it is almost always a case of Visa on Arrival, always worth checking & please don't overstay or you will be fined.

Travel Insurance: Purchase comprehensive travel insurance that covers medical emergencies, trip cancellations, and lost or stolen belongings. I don't care if you're the luckiest person in the world, get insured! Accidents are more prone to happen when travelling. Also, I'm guessing that epic volcano adventure trek isn't your weekly go-to back home.

Health & Safety is often overlooked and in some countries is inadequate. Pro tip is to make sure you get Travel Insurance in your home country, or you will be paying up to 3x more. If staying out for longer than a year (or you have ignored the above), then safetywing.com is a trusted website I have used before.

Vaccinations and Health Precautions: Check with your healthcare provider for necessary vaccinations and health advice. Central America is generally safe in this regard. Diphtheria; Hepatitis A; Rabies & Tetanus are ones to consider if you wanna be 'extra' cautious. Carry a basic first aid kit too.

Budget and Finances: Establish a realistic budget for your trip and carry a mix of cash and travel cards (Revolut & Monzo are my go-to's here). Have a separate supply of USD, all countries recognise the value, even at borders. El Salvador uses this as its main currency too!

Packing Essentials: Pack lightweight, versatile clothing suitable for various climates. Depending on time of year you'll most likely be needing clothes for hotter climates, but if travelling to rainforest regions such as in Costa Rica, a raincoat is also advised. Don't forget essentials like a sturdy backpack, travel-sized toiletries, a quick-dry towel, and a universal adapter. Dear God, bring 2 if you have the space, and plenty of spare cables too!

Emergency Contacts and Important Documents: Keep a copy of your passport, travel insurance, and emergency contacts in a separate location. Consider digital backups on a cloud/ email, and share relevant information with someone back home. Your passport is your most prized possession, and if given the chance it will be stolen. Always keep in a very secure location, only using when required. No use for nightclub ID entry please.

Local Customs and Culture: Research and respect the local customs and etiquette of the countries you'll be visiting, there's nothing worse than a rude tourist!

Language: JUST. LEARN. SPANISH! It's so important I'm adding in a specific Chapter just for it! I'm not saying you need to be able to explain to me the intricacies of a day to day. Focus on numbers, basic conjugations and conversational phrases, the rest will come, I promise! The locals will appreciate the effort and you won't get ripped off as much when bartering.
Pro tip is to focus your Spanish learning on more of a Central American persuasion, most resources show European Spanish, it makes a subtle difference and locals notice this.

Security: Make sure to buy a padlock. All hostels offer lockers for these important valuables. Useful for locking your bag too when the situation requires it.

CHAPTER TWO

GUATEMALA

"The Mayan Meander"

GUATEMALA KEY CATEGORIES

Culture: Guatemala is like a cultural party where Mayan history meets Spanish colonial vibes. Imagine wandering through vibrant indigenous markets, catching traditional ceremonies, and feeling the friendliness of the locals – it's a total immersion in the Guatemalan spirit.

Sights: Get ready for some jaw-dropping moments! Picture yourself exploring the ancient Tikal ruins, hiking around the stunning Lake Atitlán, strolling through the charming streets of Antigua, and getting lost in the colours of the Chichicastenango market. Oh, and don't even think about skipping the dreamy natural pools of Semuc Champey. The Acatenengo Volcano hike (picture on previous page) was a personal highlight!

Accommodation: Where to crash? Guatemala's got it all. Whether you're feeling a cosy guesthouse in Antigua, a lakeside spot in Panajachel, or an island escape in Flores – there's a bed with your name on it.

Cuisine: Guatemalan food is a flavour explosion! Think hearty Pepián, comforting Kak'ik, and sweet Rellenitos. And street food? Tamales and garnachas are the local stars.

GUATEMALA - QUICK FACTS

Location:
Bordered by Mexico to the north and west, Belize to the northeast, Honduras to the east, and El Salvador to the southeast.

Capital:
Guatemala City

Population:
Around 17 million people (2022)

Official Language:
Spanish, with many indigenous languages spoken, including K'iche', Kaqchikel, Q'eqchi', and Mam.

Government:
Constitutional democratic republic

Major Religion:
Predominantly Roman Catholic, with a significant indigenous influence on religious practices.

Geography:
Diverse landscapes including mountains, rainforests, and coastal plains.

Economy:
Agriculture, textiles, and tourism are significant contributors to the economy.

Cultural Heritage:
Rich indigenous culture with a blend of Spanish influences, visible in art, music, and traditional clothing.

GUATEMALA PICTURES

STEPHEN LEONARD, 2022

CHAPTER THREE

BELIZE

"The Caribbean Crusade"

BELIZE KEY CATEGORIES

Culture: Now, let's jump over to Belize, where the culture is a fantastic mix of Mayan, Creole, Garifuna, and Mestizo influences. Feel the laid-back Caribbean vibe and get ready for some serious friendliness from the Belizean people.

Sights: Belize is a visual treat! Explore the ancient Maya city of Caracol, dive into the mesmerizing Great Blue Hole, and trek through the jungle wonders of Cockscomb Basin Wildlife Sanctuary. Then, discover the unique Garifuna culture in Dangriga and chill on the laid-back beaches of Placencia. The island of Caye Caulker also offers a chilled back vibe, with their personal motto of 'go slow' it's the ideal place to spend a few days and simply relax. The snorkeling isn't bad too!

Accommodation: Belize has your stay covered, no matter your vibe. From luxurious beachfront resorts on Ambergris Caye to eco-friendly lodges in the jungle, or a more inland experience in San Ignacio – take your pick.

Cuisine: Belizean food is a taste journey! Try the classic rice and beans with stewed chicken, dive into conch fritters, and savour the goodness of hudut, a Garifuna fish and coconut stew. Street food cravings? Fry jacks and garnaches are calling your name.

BELIZE - QUICK FACTS

Location:
Bordered by Mexico to the northwest, Guatemala to the west and south, and the Caribbean Sea to the east.

Capital:
Belmopan

Population:
Around 400,000 people (2022)

Official Language:
English, with Belizean Creole, Spanish, and indigenous languages also spoken.

Government:
Constitutional monarchy and parliamentary democracy

Major Religion:
Predominantly Roman Catholic, with a diverse religious landscape.

Geography:
Diverse landscapes including coastal plains, mountains, and the Belize Barrier Reef.

Economy:
Relies on agriculture, tourism, and services.

Cultural Heritage:
Rich mix of Mayan, Garifuna, Mestizo, Creole, and other cultures, reflected in music, dance, and traditional crafts.

BELIZE PICTURES

CHAPTER FOUR

EL SALVADOR

"The Surfing Sensation"

EL SALVADOR KEY CATEGORIES

Culture: El Salvador is like a cultural fiesta, where indigenous roots and Spanish vibes create this awesome mix. Imagine diving into lively local markets, catching traditional ceremonies, and feeling the genuine friendliness of the Salvadoran crowd. The country has had a troubled history with Gangs which under their new president they are rapidly leaving behind.

Sights: Get ready for some mind-blowing moments Picture yourself wandering through the "Pompeii of the Americas," the UNESCO-listed Joya de Cerén. Hike up the impressive Santa Ana volcano (I can safely say Santa Ana's blue volcano is the only one I've ever seen in my life!) Catch some waves on the Pacific beaches of El Tunco & El Zonte which feature stunning beaches. They were also where I upped my surfing level at a very affordable rate Or choose to take a leisurely stroll through the charming towns along the flower-filled Ruta de las Flores.

Accommodation: El Salvador's got your back when it comes to crashing. Whether you're into boutique hotels with that extra charm or beachside hostels for those laid-back vibes, you'll find your spot. Cosy guesthouses feature up and down the beachfront, with unlimited places to relax & surf.

Cuisine: Now, let's talk about foodie delights! Pepián, a hearty meat stew, is like a warm hug for your taste buds Kak'ik, the turkey soup, is a personal game-changer. And Rellenitos? Sweet plantain desserts that'll have you craving more. Hit up the street food markets for tamales and garnachas – you won't be disappointed!

EL SALVADOR - QUICK FACTS

Location:
Bordered by Honduras to the northeast, Guatemala to the northwest, and the Pacific Ocean to the south.

Capital:
San Salvador

Population:
Around 6.5 million people (2022)

Official Language:
Spanish, with a significant portion of the population being bilingual in Spanish and indigenous languages.

Government:
Unitary presidential republic

Major Religion:
Predominantly Roman Catholic, with a growing Protestant minority.

Geography:
Mostly mountainous with a narrow coastal belt.

Economy:
Heavily reliant on the services sector and remittances from Salvadorans living abroad.

Cultural Heritage:
Rich cultural traditions influenced by indigenous and Spanish roots, reflected in art, literature, and traditional celebrations.

EL SALVADOR PICTURES

CHAPTER FIVE

HONDURAS

"The Scuba Stunner"

HONDURAS KEY CATEGORIES

Culture: Jumping over to Honduras, the culture is a vibrant canvas painted with indigenous vibes, Spanish flair, and a sprinkle of Garifuna magic along the Caribbean coast. Dive into local traditions, check out the colourful Lenca pottery, and explore the historical charm of places like Comayagua.

Sights: Honduras is a visual feast! Explore the ancient Maya city of Copán, where the stone carvings will blow your mind. Snorkel or dive in the turquoise waters around the Bay Islands, soak in the colonial vibes of Gracias, and lose yourself in the lush landscapes of Pico Bonito National Park. The islands of Roatán & Utila are some of the best in the world to get your scuba diving certificates at a great price. I got lost in the beauty of Roatán for close to a week in my visit!

Accommodation: Honduras has a spot for every traveller. From eco-lodges surrounded by nature to beach resorts that scream paradise, you'll find your perfect crash pad. Copán's got these adorable boutique hotels, and the Bay Islands offer beachfront options for that tropical getaway.

Cuisine: Let's talk about Honduran flavours! Baleadas, those folded tortillas with beans and cheese, are a must-try. Super filling too. Sopa de Caracol, a conch soup, will warm your soul, and Tapado, a coconut seafood stew, is immense. And don't even think about passing up the street food scene – empanadas and tamales are calling your name!

HONDURAS - QUICK FACTS

Location:
Bordered by Guatemala to the west, El Salvador to the southwest, Nicaragua to the southeast, the Gulf of Honduras to the north, and the Pacific Ocean to the south.

Capital:
Tegucigalpa

Population:
Around 10 million people (2022)

Official Language:
Spanish, with indigenous languages spoken by various ethnic groups.

Government:
Unitary presidential republic

Major Religion:
Predominantly Roman Catholic, with a growing Protestant minority.

Geography:
Diverse landscapes, including mountains, coastal areas, and the Mosquito Coast.

Economy:
Relies on agriculture, manufacturing, and services. Remittances from Hondurans abroad are also significant.

Cultural Heritage:
Influenced by indigenous, African, and Spanish cultures, reflected in music, dance, and traditional crafts.

HONDURAS PICTURES

STEPHEN LEONARD, 2022

CHAPTER SIX

NICARAGUA

"The Volcano Venture"

NICARAGUA KEY CATEGORIES

Culture: Nicaragua is a real mix of traditions! You'll feel the warmth of the locals as you explore bustling markets, catch traditional dances, and dive into the country's fascinating history. From indigenous roots to Spanish colonial influences, there's a rich tapestry of culture to discover.

Sights: Picture yourself strolling through the charming colonial streets of Granada and León, or hiking up volcanoes like Concepción and Maderas on Ometepe Island. Want a beach day? San Juan del Sur's pristine beaches are calling. And don't miss the Islets of Granada – tiny islands with big character on Lake Nicaragua. Volcan Masaya featured on the previous page features scenes straight from Mount Doom.

Accommodation: Your stay can be as eclectic as the culture. Choose between boutique hotels in Granada, cosy spots or full nature living on Ometepe Island (cheeky picture included of my rainforest accommodation). There are also amazing beachside hostels in San Juan del Sur. Each place has its own vibe, reflecting Nicaragua's diverse offerings.

Cuisine: Food in Nicaragua is a flavour party! Try gallo pinto, a local favorite of rice and beans. For a hearty meal, there's vigorón – cabbage and yuca with pork. Seafood lovers, you're in for a treat along the coasts. And don't forget to snack on quesillo and explore the tasty world of fritangas.

NICARAGUA - QUICK FACTS

Location:
Bordered by Honduras to the north, Costa Rica to the south, the Caribbean Sea to the east, and the Pacific Ocean to the west.

Capital:
Managua

Population:
Around 6.5 million people (2022)

Official Language:
Spanish, with indigenous languages spoken by various ethnic groups.

Government:
Presidential republic

Major Religion:
Predominantly Roman Catholic, with a growing Protestant minority.

Geography:
Diverse landscapes, including volcanoes, lakes, and coastal areas.

Economy:
Agriculture, mining, and services are significant contributors to the economy.

Cultural Heritage:
Influenced by indigenous cultures, African heritage, and Spanish colonisation, reflected in music, dance, and traditional celebrations.

23

NICARAGUA PICTURES

CHAPTER SEVEN

COSTA RICA

"The Rainforest Roam"

COSTA RICA KEY CATEGORIES

Culture: Costa Rica is all about "Pura Vida" – a lifestyle embracing nature, friendliness, and joy. Dive into local markets, soak up the vibe in San José, and join in on traditional celebrations. The commitment to biodiversity is part of the culture here, and lets not forget about the famous sloth!

Sights: Get ready for a nature extravaganza! Explore Manuel Antonio and Tortuguero, where diverse ecosystems come to life. Hike the Arenal Volcano, swing through the treetops in Monteverde, and relax on the golden beaches of Tamarindo. Get your full rainforest fix at Cahuita National Park. Costa Rica is like a living postcard.

Accommodation: Whether you're into eco-lodges surrounded by nature in Monteverde or seaside resorts in Tamarindo, Costa Rica's got your stay covered. The accommodations here are as diverse as the landscapes, offering a bit of luxury or a touch of rustic charm.

Cuisine: Let's talk about foodie delights! Casado is a must-try – rice, beans, plantains, and your choice of protein. Seafood lovers will revel in ceviche, and the streets are alive with the tempting aroma of empanadas and tamales. Don't forget to snack on the abundance of tropical fruits.

COSTA RICA - QUICK FACTS

Location:
Bordered by Nicaragua to the north, Panama to the southeast, the Pacific Ocean to the west, and the Caribbean Sea to the east.

Capital:
San José

Population:
Around 5 million people (2022)

Official Language:
Spanish

Government:
Unitary presidential republic

Major Religion:
Predominantly Roman Catholic, with a growing Protestant minority.

Geography:
Diverse landscapes, including mountains, coastal plains, and rainforests.

Economy:
Tourism, agriculture, and technology are major components of the economy.

Cultural Heritage:
Rich cultural traditions influenced by indigenous, European, and African roots, reflected in music, dance, and traditional festivals.

COSTA RICA PICTURES

CHAPTER EIGHT

PANAMA

"The Urban Undertaking"

PANAMA KEY CATEGORIES

Culture: Panama is a cool fusion of old and new, nature and urbanisation. You've got the indigenous traditions mixing it up with Spanish influences, and don't forget the Afro-Caribbean vibes on the coast. Dive into the local culture, catch some folkloric dances, and embrace the laid-back yet vibrant atmosphere. The famous Panama hat is everywhere you go too!

Sights: First up, the Panama Canal – an engineering marvel you can't miss. Wander through the historic streets of Casco Viejo, a UNESCO World Heritage site with its colourful buildings and lively squares. For nature lovers, the cloud forests of Boquete and the stunning beaches of Bocas del Toro are must-sees.

Accommodation: Panama's got your back when it comes to staying comfy. Casco Viejo offers charming boutique hotels, while Bocas del Toro has these adorable beachfront bungalows. Panama City, with its skyscrapers and historic sites, provides a range of options for all tastes.

Cuisine: Try the iconic sancocho, a hearty chicken soup that warms the soul. Seafood lovers, don't miss the ceviche, especially on the coastal areas. And the empanadas? Pure deliciousness in a crunchy package.

PANAMA - QUICK FACTS

Location:
Bordered by Costa Rica to the west, Colombia to the southeast, the Caribbean Sea to the north, and the Pacific Ocean to the south.

Capital:
Panama City

Population:
Around 4 million people (2022)

Official Language:
Spanish

Government:
Unitary presidential republic

Major Religion:
Predominantly Roman Catholic, with a significant Protestant minority.

Geography:
Diverse landscapes, including mountains, rainforests, and coastal areas.

Economy:
Strategic location with a focus on services, trade, and finance. The Panama Canal is a crucial part of global trade.

Cultural Heritage:
Influenced by indigenous cultures, Spanish colonisation, and Afro-Caribbean traditions.

PANAMA PICTURES

STEPHEN LEONARD, 2022

CHAPTER NINE

HOSTEL HACKS

Hostel Room Size: A larger hostel dorm is a wallet-friendly choice, offering the most economical paid accommo. If Couchsurfing isn't your cup of tea, this is the next best route to save money on your lodging. The rule of thumb here: the bigger the dorm, the lighter on your pocket. While a 4-6 bed dorm might provide a bit more privacy, stretching your budget is more attainable in a 12-18 bed one. Over time, these savings can really add up. Pack your earplugs and a sleeping mask, and embrace the cost-effective allure of the larger dorms!

Hostel Reviews: Most answers can be found in those hostel comments! For the light sleepers among us, dive into the reviews before booking to dodge the party hostel scene. In bustling cities, you'll likely stumble upon a quieter hostel option. It might sacrifice some social aspects or central location, but the promise of a good night's sleep is worth it. Pick and choose for the kind of vibe you're feeling.

Prep your own meals: The key to stretching your travel budget that bit further is to whip up your own meals. During my time in Central America, by no means did I avoid eating out, quite the opposite. A bit of research & shopping local gave me the balance of a healthy home-cooked meal and sampling the regional delicacies.

Hostel Kitchens: If you're crashing in hostels, opt for those with a kitchen facility. That way, you've got the perfect setup for some culinary adventures. With Couchsurfing or Airbnb, chances are your host will provide kitchen access.

No kitchen? No problem. Toss in your own container and cutlery, and whip up some delicious sandwiches and salads on the fly. After all, not every meal requires a hob.

Remember, just because you're on the move doesn't mean you're obliged to dine out for every meal. Skipping a restaurant visit won't put a dampener on your trip!

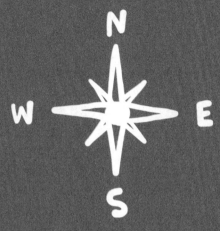

CHAPTER TEN

EXPLORING ADVICE

Opting to walk: Central America is abundant in smaller locations ripe for exploring by foot. Apart from keeping a low carbon footprint, walking also gives you a greater opportunity to meet locals & lets you dive right into local life. You can chat with people, see how they live day-to-day, and really get a feel for the culture.

Walking Tours: Keen to discover the city, familiarise yourself with its layout, and check out the key attractions? Opt for a complimentary walking tour. These are readily available in most major cities – inquire at the local tourist office, chat with your hostel staff, or simply Google "free walking tour (city name)."

Flexibility: No strict schedules, no waiting for the next bus – you decide the pace. Want to spend an extra hour at that quirky street market? Go for it. Walking gives you the freedom to be your own travel boss.

Embrace the Siesta Culture: Central America loves its siestas. Depending on which time of year you visit, Midday can be pretty quiet, so use that time to soak in the atmosphere. Enjoy a leisurely lunch, sip on some local coffee, and just chill. It's the perfect time to people-watch.

Art and Murals Galore: Keep an eye out for street art and murals. Central American cities are like open-air galleries. Each splash of color tells a story. It's a cool way to feel the vibe of a place.

Check Out Local Events: Central America loves to party! Keep an ear out for local events, festivals, or parades during your visit. Joining in on the celebrations is an instant ticket to the heart of the community.

Street Food: Central America is a street food paradise! Try local bites from street vendors. It's not just about the food; it's a cultural experience Pupusas in El Salvador or baleadas in Honduras are a personal go-to – you'll thank me later!

36

CHAPTER ELEVEN

GENERAL TIPS & TRICKS

Be Open to Change: Plans are great, but so is spontaneity. Research & planning are not the same thing! Embrace change, go with the flow, and be open to new experiences. Some of the best adventures happen when you least expect it.

Safety First: Trust your instincts. If a situation doesn't feel right, it probably isn't. Keep an eye on your belongings, and use lockers in hostels. Central America has dangers like all countries, and tourists can be major targets. To reference an experience that happened with me, if there are protests on the streets then it may be a good idea to skip an attraction that day.

Stay Hydrated: It sounds basic, but it's crucial. Keep a water bottle handy, especially in warmer climates. Dehydration is not your travel buddy. Depending how far off the beaten track you're going an extra tip can be carrying some iodine tablets or a bottle with a filtration system.

Meet Other Travellers: Backpacking is a social game. Don't be shy – strike up conversations with fellow backpackers. You might find travel buddies, share tips, or discover new destinations. Someone who has recently experienced the area you have just arrived in will give you a better breakdown than any book or site. They can also save you wasted journeys & invaluable advice on mistakes they've made.

Pack Light, Pack Right: Seriously, less is more. You're the one lugging that backpack around, so stick to the essentials. You'll thank yourself when you're breezing through crowded stations and narrow streets.

Use Offline Maps: Download offline maps before you venture out. This way, even if you lose Wi-Fi or data, you can still navigate your way through the streets. Also, get used to Google or Apple maps if you do have Internet, it's an everyday-use item for sure.

Backup Your Photos: Losing your photos can be heartbreaking. Regularly back up your pictures to cloud storage or an external device. You'll thank yourself if anything happens to your camera or phone.

Invest in Quality Gear: Your backpack, shoes, and other gear are your constant companions. Invest in quality items that will last. Uncomfortable shoes or a failing zipper can quickly become your worst enemy.

Have a Local SIM Card: This one relates to the Maps advice on the previous page! A local SIM can save you from hefty international roaming charges. Having a local number also makes it easier to get in touch with locals or local businesses.

Have a Positive Attitude: Things won't always go smoothly, and that's okay. Approach challenges with a positive attitude and a sense of humour. It's all part of the adventure. You will likely experience home sickness too, it will pass, I promise!

Capture Moments, Not Just Photos: It's not just about snapping pics for Insta. Sometimes the best memories are the ones you don't capture on camera. Queue cringey advice about *actually* being in the moment, just try it before rolling your eyes at me!

Join Travel Communities: Online travel communities and forums are gold mines. Connect with fellow travellers, ask questions, and share your experiences. Hostelworld, which I mainly use for my stays recently added a chat function, super useful for all things travel!!

Emergency Stash: Keep a small emergency stash of local currency. It might come in handy when you least expect it – like when you arrive late at night and the ATMs are playing hide and seek. As mentioned at the start, USD is King here.

Stay Hygienic on the Go: Wet wipes, hand sanitiser, and a quick-dry towel are your hygiene superheroes.

Currencies:

- Guatemala: Guatemalan Quetzal (GTQ)
- El Salvador: United States Dollar (USD)
- Honduras: Honduran Lempira (HNL)
- Nicaragua: Nicaraguan Córdoba (NIO)
- Costa Rica: Costa Rican Colón (CRC)
- Panama: Panamanian Balboa (PAB) and United States Dollar (USD)
- Belize: Belize Dollar (BZD)

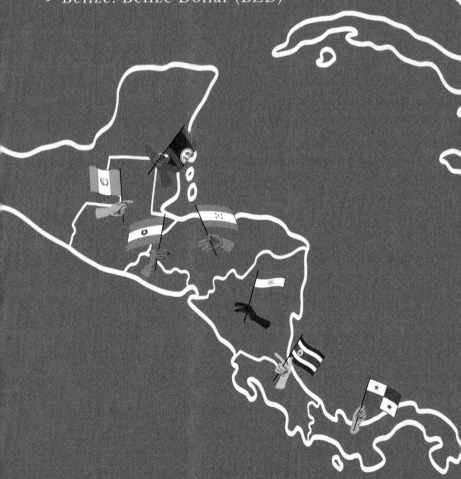

la vida bonita

STEPHEN'S SPANISH BASICS

Why you should learn some Spanish before visiting:

Spanish Speaking countries in Central America:
As you've now (hopefully) learnt from previous sections, of the 7 countries in Central America, 6 of these speak Spanish as the main language. The exception is Belize which speaks English due to its history as a British colony, Spanish is readily understood here though too (so it's basically all 7 right!?)

Central American Spanish: As I touched on earlier, the Spanish spoken in these countries is different to your usual Spanish. In Spain 'coger' means to take, but in Central America .. well lets just learn the basics first! ;)

Feel More Secure: Knowing the local language can contribute to a sense of security. It reduces the likelihood of misunderstandings and helps you navigate situations with confidence.

Enjoy a More Authentic Experience: Learning the language allows you to step off the beaten path and experience the daily life of locals. You can engage in conversations beyond the basic tourist script and discover hidden gems suggested by the people who know the area best.

Negotiate and Shop Smart: This one should not be underrated! Haggling is a common practice in many Central American markets. Knowing Spanish allows you to negotiate confidently, ensuring you get fair prices on goods and services.

On the next few pages I'll provide you with basic Spanish Phrases which I have found the most useful. This is by no means extensive but should provide a good foundation for you to continue on your own Spanish learning journey!

Spanish Basic Phrases:

Greetings:
Hello - Hola
Good morning - Buenos días
Good afternoon - Buenas tardes
Good evening/night - Buenas noches

How are you? - ¿Cómo estás? (informal) / ¿Cómo está usted? (formal)
- You'll find most interactions in Central America use informal Spanish, although save the formal for that extra special person you want to impress!

Common Courtesy:
Please - Por favor
Thank you - Gracias
You're welcome - De nada
Excuse me / I'm sorry - Perdón / Lo siento

Basic Communication:
Yes - Sí
No - No
Maybe - Quizás / Tal vez
I don't understand - No entiendo
I don't speak much Spanish - No hablo mucho español
Can you help me? - ¿Puede(s) ayudarme?

Directions:
Where is...? - ¿Dónde está...?
Left - Izquierda
Right - Derecha
Straight ahead - Todo recto
Stop - Alto

Numbers:
This one deserves its own page. Seriously, if you choose to master one aspect of this chapter, this is it. Once I had my numbers down, every interaction just seemed a little bit smoother and less stressful. Get practicing!

- 1 – uno
- 2 – dos
- 3 – tres
- 4 – cuatro
- 5 – cinco
- 6 – seis
- 7 – siete
- 8 – ocho
- 9 – nueve
- 10 – diez
- 11 – once
- 12 – doce
- 13 – trece
- 14 – catorce
- 15 – quince
- 16 – dieciséis
- 17 – diecisiete
- 18 – dieciocho
- 19 – diecinueve
- 20 – veinte

- 30 - treinta
- 40 - cuarenta
- 50 - cincuenta
- 60 - sesenta
- 70 - setenta
- 80 - ochenta
- 90 - noventa
- 100 - cien

- 200 - doscientos
- 300 - trescientos
- 400 - cuatrocientos
- 500 - quinientos
- 600 - seiscientos
- 700 - setecientos
- 800 - ochocientos
- 900 - novecientos
- 1000 - mil

Common Travel Phrases:
I need a hostel/ hotel - Necesito un hostal/ hotel
Where is the bathroom? - ¿Dónde está el baño?
How much does this cost? - ¿Cuánto cuesta esto?
I would like... - Me gustaría...
Can I have the check, please? - ¿La cuenta, por favor?

Emergencies:
Help! - ¡Ayuda!
I need a doctor - Necesito un médico
I'm lost - Estoy perdido/a
I've lost my passport - He perdido mi pasaporte

(If you follow my above tips hopefully this isn't you!
Always best to have it memorised for worst case
scenarios though)

Food and Dining:
Menu - Menú
Water - Agua
Food - Comida
Delicious - Delicioso/a
I'm a vegetarian - Soy vegetariano/a

Shopping:
How much is this? - ¿Cuánto cuesta esto?
Do you accept credit/ debit cards? - ¿Aceptan tarjetas
de crédito/ débito?

Authors Note

Firstly, I sincerely hope you enjoy this book! It's been over a year in the making and if it helps just ONE person have a more enjoyable and fulfilling experience in Central America, it will all have been worth it! Special mention to my friend Amira who helped me with the picture selection and placement, something that I really suck at!

I have kept things deliberately light on the sections of Culture, Sights, Accommodation and Cuisine. Like the title states, this book is a 'Guide' and should be treated as such. The recommendations are based on real people's own thoughts & experiences, which I have carefully picked up along my journey. Therefore, you may feel differently and that's ok! My advice would be to take a look and see which aspects resonate more with you. I've found the Central American experiences are best savoured and undertaken at a leisurely pace.

For me, the true beauty of travelling is in experiencing the day to day. It's great to research and to plan, but don't overdo it. In my years of travelling I have found the more granular you go, the less you can just soak up a moment, and not have to worry about what comes next. This is the true feeling which keeps me travelling and always seeking out my next adventure!

I have added in additional pages for notes. My dream is for this to be a worthy travel companion for someone journeying through Central America. I often find with other guides there is a lack of space for notes, and details can quickly be forgotten. Please treat this section however you wish, add your thoughts, experiences, hidden gems, journaling or just doodle a smiley face if the mood takes you. It's yours to do as you wish.

Thanks for reading and keep adventuring always!
Stephen

Notes

Notes

Notes

Notes

Notes

Notes

Notes

Notes

Notes

Notes

Notes

Notes

Notes

Notes

Notes

Notes

Notes

Notes

Notes

Notes

Notes

Notes

Notes

Notes

Notes

Notes

Printed in Great Britain
by Amazon

37694052R10046